ideals®
FRIENDSHIP

JULY 2004

Dedicated to a celebration of the American ideals of faith in God, loyalty to country, and love of family.

Friendship . . . with the exception of wisdom, no better thing has been given to man. —Cicero

IDEALS—Vol 61, No. 4 July 2004 IDEALS (ISSN 0019-137X, USPS 256-240) is published six times a year: January, March, May, July, September, and November by IDEALS PUBLICATIONS, a division of Guideposts, 39 Seminary Hill Road, Carmel, NY 10512. Copyright © 2004 by IDEALS PUBLICATIONS, a division of Guideposts. All rights reserved. The cover and entire contents of IDEALS are fully protected by copyright and must not be reproduced in any manner whatsoever. Title IDEALS registered U.S. Patent Office. Printed and bound in USA by Quebecor Printing. Printed on Weyerhaeuser Husky. The paper used in this publication meets the minimum requirements of American National Standard for Information Sciences—Permanence of Paper for Printed Library Materials, ANSI Z39.48-1984. Periodicals postage paid at Carmel, New York, and additional mailing offices. Canadian mailed under Publications Mail Agreement Number 40010140. POSTMASTER: Send address changes to Ideals, 39 Seminary Hill Road, Carmel, NY 10512. CANADA POST: Send address changes to Guideposts PO Box 1051, Fort Erie ON L2A 6C7. For subscription or customer service questions, contact Ideals Publications, a division of Guideposts, 39 Seminary Hill Road, Carmel, NY 10512. Fax 845-228-2115. Reader Preference Service: We occasionally make our mailing lists available to other companies whose products or services might interest you. If you prefer not to be included, please write to Ideals Customer Service.

ISBN 0-8249-1233-0 GST 893989236

Visit the *Ideals* website at www.idealsbooks.com

Cover: A lovely invitation to relax and enjoy the warm outdoors with a special friend is presented in this photograph by Nancy Matthews.

Inside front cover: Two young ladies share a quiet moment in the garden in this painting by Guerenadi (Gennadi) Bernadsky, entitled UNDER THE BIRCH TREES. Image provided by Fine Art Photographic Library, Ltd., London/Bourne Gallery Reigate/Art Gallery Gerard Wassenaar.

Inside back cover: The bounty of summer is portrayed in this exquisite painting by Jan Van Os (1744–1808), entitled A RICH STILL LIFE OF SUMMER FLOWERS. Image provided by Fine Art Photographic Library, Ltd., London/John Mitchell & Sons.

In This Issue

Summer Sun
Robert Louis Stevenson

Great is the sun, and wide he goes
Through empty heaven without repose;
And in the blue and glowing days,
More thick than rain he showers his rays.

Though closer still the blinds we pull
To keep the shady parlor cool,
Yet he will find a chink or two
To slip his golden fingers through.

The dusty attic, spider-clad,
He, through the keyhole, maketh glad
And through the broken edge of tiles
Into the laddered hayloft smiles.

Meantime his golden face around
He bares to all the garden ground
And sheds a warm and glittering look
Among the ivy's inmost nook.

Above the hills, along the blue,
Round the bright air with footing true,
To please the child, to paint the rose,
The gardener of the world, he goes.

August
Helen Virden

August, now, and sun pours
Golden radiance on the earth;
The clover in the ripened fields
Is measuring its full green worth.

Now food is in the grain,
Thirsty grass spins out its gold,
Each day is burnished copper,
The once-young year grows old.

The sun burns low;
And then, beyond the hedge,
The moon comes slowly up,
A silver coin clipped on the edge.

The Virgin River flows past cottonwoods in the canyon at the Gateway to the Narrows in Zion National Park, Utah. Photograph by Terry Donnelly/Donnelly Austin Photography.

Sound of Summer
Ruby Lee Mitchell

The hazy veil of evening,
Dotted with soft-glowing fireflies,
Drapes the earth with sweet enchantment
As the long day fades and then dies.

Flowers offer their fragrant incense,
In the dusk of a smoke-blue twilight,
To the mystery and the magic—
Fair acolytes to the waiting night.

So still the air and still the wonder,
With beauty holding one spellbound,
Feeling summer's soft, warm breathing
And listening to its gentle sound.

Summer Melodies
Lillian Busby

Return, sweet summer melodies,
And fill my days with your bright glow;
You travel on the kindly breeze,
But where you start, I cannot go.

Bring me the drone of motorboats,
The sighs of trains across damp air,
The happy chant of wild bird notes,
The sound of streams that eddy there.

Return, sweet summer melodies,
Sing through the hours, your strains prolong,
With light and rest my heart appease,
Enfold me in exquisite song.

Summer
Edna Gerstner

Hammock time is enticing;
Tip your face up to the sky.
Join me in cataloging clouds;
Overhead they shuffle by.
Energetic other seasons,
Fall and winter and the spring,
Stimulate, but summer whispers,
"Why, oh, why do anything?"
So I swing here in my hammock,
Anchored safe upon the fence,
And sing a serenade to summer's
Lovely days of indolence.

Summer Symphony
Lynda Schlomann

I wish on the stars above me
As a crescent moon swings low;
I receive the evening's benediction
Wrapped in the sunset's afterglow.

I glory in the exultant sky
That spills the sudden rain,
As the brook flows on with a purling sound
Through a meadow that is fresh again.

The altar hills await to echo
The bird on a swinging branch,
As from his happy throat he pours
The notes of a golden avalanche.

The gates of His house are open;
The red rose points the way,
Because heaven always seems nearer
On a beautiful summer day.

Fireweed, paintbrush, and cow parsnip flourish on a ridge above the Valley of the Ten Peaks, Moraine Creek, and Mount Babel in Banff National Park, Canada, with the Wenkchemna Peaks in the background. Photograph by Mary Liz Austin/Donnelly Austin Photography.

Mid-August

Louise Driscoll

Spiders are spinning their webs;
I hear pears softly falling;
Birds are so still; yesterday
They were singing, calling.

Grapes are swelling now,
Globes of silver-green.
Their leaves lie close, but
The sun slips in between.

There's a blue haze in the air;
A butterfly's questing flight
Leads where petunias bloom,
Crimson and mauve and white.

The goldfinch sits like a jewel
By dried hollyhock seeds;
The wayside is adorned,
Vivid with full-grown weeds.

The fields are dappled brown;
The barns are filled
And sweet with hay that spills
Clover distilled.

August is a quiet time.
Do you hear the pears fall?
Cicadas all day long
Flute a humming call.

Crossed Threads

Helen Jackson

The silken threads by viewless spinners spun,
Which float so idly on the summer air
And help to make each summer morning fair,
Shining like silver in the summer sun,
Are caught by wayward breezes, one by one,
And blown to east and west and fastened there,
Weaving on all the roads their sudden snare.
No sign which road doth safest, freest run,
The winged insects know, that soar so gay
To meet their death upon each summer day.
How dare we any human deed arraign,
Attempt to reckon any moment's cost,
Or any pathway trust as safe and plain
Because we see not where the threads have crossed?

Morning dew bejewels a spider web near Lubec, Maine.
Photograph by Dick Dietrich/Dietrich Leis Stock Photography.

August Wind
Kathleen Clark

August wind,
omnipresent,
sucking my breath . . .
basking in summer's sauna,
crickets' and cicadas'
miniature motors
strum, throb, and whirr
a symphony
heard by those who dwell
under the green canopy.
Lazy August wind lulls me into
the pulse of the night,
and my spirit is renewed
to hear the mirth
of the dew-cooled earth.
Against the midnight blue curtain,
silver stars wink
radio messages,
fluorescently blinking fireflies
jet through the air
in criss-cross formations,
and in treetops
katydids vibrate
with night songs.

Star Light, Star Bright
Bettie M. Sellers

Standing on the edge of the farm's faint glow,
I spoke my secrets to the dark country sky.
Hailing that great inconceivable distance,
Jubilant with tiny winking lights,
I almost believed that I could charm one
To my hands, rub it like a genie's lamp,
And see my wishes appear, suddenly shimmering,
Jeweled out of the night.

Summertime
Marjorie Martin

Beneath the shade of willow trees,
Summer hours are spent at ease,
Watching cloudlets in the sky
Mirrored in the stream nearby,
Allowing the song of the whippoorwill
To give my heart a summertime thrill—
Lovely, golden August day,
A time to dream, a time to play.

Day lilies and a birdhouse add cheerful color to a country fence in Floyds Knobs, Indiana. Photograph by Daniel Dempster.

Summer Saturday

Eileen Spinelli

I like walking
past your house
like I'm on my way
to somewhere.

I like catching you there
in the front yard
watering daisies.

I like when you see me,
when you wave
and smile.

For a little while
then
on a summer Saturday,
the whole world
is a poem
and my heart
the last line
of it.

Summer Days
Wathen Marks Wilks Call

In summer, when the days were long,
We walked, two friends, in field and wood;
Our heart was light, our step was strong,
And life lay round us, fair as good,
In summer, when the days were long.

We strayed from morn till evening came.
We gathered flowers and wove us crowns;
We walked mid poppies red as flame
Or sat upon the yellow downs
And always wished our life the same.

In summer, when the days were long,
We leaped the hedgerow, crossed the brook;
And still her voice flowed forth in song,
Or else she read some graceful book,
In summer, when the days were long.

In summer, when the days were long,
We plucked wild strawberries, ripe and red,
Or feasted, with no grace but song,
On golden nectar, snow-white bread,
In summer, when the days were long.

We loved, and yet we knew it not,
For loving seemed like breathing then;
We found a heaven in every spot;
Saw angels, too, in all good men,
And dreamed of gods in grove and grot.

In summer, when the days are long,
I love her as I loved of old;
My heart is light, my step is strong,
For love brings back those hours of gold,
In summer, when the days are long.

Two bicycles are parked in front of Crane Cottage,
Jekyll Island, Georgia, on a sunny summer day.
Photograph by William H. Johnson.

Who Strive Their Best

Florence Marie Taylor

The gentleness of August days
    is in the wind that fingers
    little butterballs of clouds.
Beside the road, for passersby,
    masses of Queen Anne's lace
    strew flower stars.
The willow bends within the quietness,
    her long green skirts
    hung lank to shade a nest.
Crawdads are sheltered by thick river weeds
    along the shallow depths
    that edge the stream.
Late shadows lengthen;
    horizon pines
    receive the sun.
Small farm homes dot
    the twilight like
    white cherry blossoms.
Night comes on
    led by a star.
    Both man and the day
Who strived their best
    retire contentedly
    to grateful rest.

Wild Asters

Herta Rosenblatt

Someone whose heart sang joy
Walked through my garden;
Was it night with only the moon to know?
I found the love song where the notes had fallen,
Blooming in a thousand stars where yesterday
The glory of the earth shone red and gold.
Who came, so still, and left for me this heaven?

Rendezvous

Sylvia Auxier

Late-blooming asters,
We call you "Farewell, Summer,"
For you are the last to lay your pale
Colors for her approval,
Steal a bit of the sky,
Hold it fast in your petals,
And wait for me in the forgotten road
Where the treetops cross.
I will outwit November's wind
And meet you there,
For I have a lake of the sky
Hidden in my heart:
We will remember Summer together.

A field near Alexandria, New Hampshire, offers a beautiful setting for a woodland walk. Photograph by William H. Johnson.

FROM MY GARDEN JOURNAL

Lisa Ragan

AGAPANTHUS

Many American gardeners crave a touch of the tropics in their gardens and will go to great lengths to achieve it. They'll even coddle a specimen in a pot all summer and then lug it to the garage for the winter, only to see their tropical beauty die before spring. And I admit, I've done my share of lugging. But this year I've become enchanted with *Agapanthus*, a blue-blossomed exotic that now includes many hardy varieties and cultivars that will withstand winters in the ground.

Agapanthus hails from South Africa and made its way to European gardens in the late seventeenth century before traveling to America. Also known as the African lily, *Agapanthus* is currently classified as a member of the lily family but has also been classified in the onion family. South African botanists prefer to classify *Agapanthus* in its own family, *Agapanthaceae*. Somehow the plant became known in some regions as the Lily of the Nile; which is a complete misnomer, since the Nile River does not traverse South Africa at all. Even more confusing is the South African lily, *Clivia miniata*, which produces orange blossoms and is a different plant altogether.

"FLOWER OF LOVE"

The name *Agapanthus* has been attributed to the Greek words *agape*, "unselfish love," and *anthos*, "flower," and thus is called the "flower of love." But more recent gardeners have questioned this interpretation since the root word *agapeo* translates as "being contented with." Exotic-hungry American gardeners, however, will likely adopt the "flower of love" version when these blue beauties grace their flower beds.

The *Agapanthus* is a herbaceous perennial that grows from a thick, fleshy root called a rhizome into a leek-like plant with solid or variegated foliage ranging in hue from green to gray-green. The blossoms, which appear in midsummer and last until early fall, resemble those

AGAPANTHUS

in the onion family with their puffy balls of tiny, funnel- or bell-shaped flower clusters in colors from deep blue to pure white. *Agapanthus* cultivars also vary in size from dwarf plants of eighteen inches tall to giants of five feet high.

HYBRIDS AND CULTIVARS

Today's gardener can choose from more than fifty *Agapanthus* hybrids and cultivars, many considered hardy. Some species are evergreen while some are deciduous, meaning they drop their leaves in the winter. The deciduous species are considered the hardier of the two and can withstand colder winters. One popular deciduous species, A. *campanulatus*, includes the Headbourne hybrids, which produce three- to four-foot plants with lavender-blue blossoms. Dwarf cultivars include the eighteen-inch Peter Pan and the two-foot Tinkerbell, while giant cultivars include the four-foot Storm Cloud with its dark blue to deep violet flower heads and the evergreen Ellamae, a five-foot beauty with purplish blue blossoms. A multitude of blue-flowered varieties can be grown, including Blue Danube, Joyful Blue, and Blue Mist. *Agapanthus* plants with white flower heads include Bressingham White and White Ice.

CULTIVATION

Agapanthus flowers grow best when planted in rich, well-drained soil in full to partial sun. Rhizomes should be planted one inch deep and spaced twelve to eighteen inches apart. The plants will need heavy and frequent watering throughout the growing season and a heavy mulch of straw throughout the winter. In areas with very cold winters, *Agapanthus* will grow best if planted slightly crowded in a pot and overwintered in a garage or basement that remains above freezing. This means some lugging, but the plant performs well in pots, and the explosion of puffy blue blossoms in mid-July will be worth it.

Agapanthus can be propagated from seeds, but the recommended method is by division in the spring. Evergreen cultivars should be divided every four years, deciduous cultivars every six years. The plants often hybridize freely, so various cultivars should not be planted next to one another if they are to remain pure.

Happily, *Agapanthus* is not troubled by many pests or diseases. Deer, in fact, find the plant completely unappealing. Slugs and snails enjoy dining on the leaves and stems but will not harm a healthy plant. Likewise, red spider mites, thrips, and mealy bugs may feast on *Agapanthus* but will require spraying only if the infestation is severe. Some plants contract botrytis, which appears as brownish lesions and will require spraying before and after the buds open.

With so many varieties and cultivars to choose from, gardeners all across America can find one to suit their climate or at least know that the plant will thrive in a crowded pot on the patio. And those brilliant blue, exotic blossoms in the summer make it all worthwhile.

Lisa Ragan, with the help of her son, Trenton, tends a small but mighty garden in Nashville, Tennessee.

Sprinkling Cans
Eva Ehrman

Visiting to cheer a friend,
Chatting there a while,
Taking drops of fun and joy,
Helping grow a smile—
All are as water from a can,
Sprinkled here and there.
Human folk, like garden friends,
Need some love and care.

It's Raining
Daniel J. Brady

When it rains, I think of you;
And yes, I smile, I really do.
Some days of rain, we walked in sand
And, other times, for shelter ran.

Then there were times when raindrops fell
We rode our bikes, a fond farewell;
And through it all, we'd have such fun—
All of this, without the sun.

I hear that laughter, now and then;
It somehow says, "Remember when
The showers came, the clouds grew gray?"
I wouldn't have it any other way.

Together, where the sea meets sand,
A windy chill, a raindrop in hand,
A quiet time, the earth stood still—
I remember now and always will.

Whenever I see
The raindrops fall,
It is you I'll remember
Most of all.

Dahlias provide brilliant color in a garden at Shore Acres State Park, Oregon.
Photograph by Mary Liz Austin/Donnelly Austin Photography.

16

The proper office of a friend is to side with you when you are in the wrong.
Nearly anybody will side with you when you are in the right.

Mark Twain

The Arrow and the Song

Henry Wadsworth Longfellow

I shot an arrow into the air;
It fell to earth, I know not where;
For, so swiftly it flew, the sight
Could not follow it in its flight.

I breathed a song into the air;
It fell to earth, I know not where;
For who has sight so keen and strong
That it can follow the flight of a song?

Long, long afterward, in an oak
I found the arrow, still unbroke;
And the song, from beginning to end,
I found again in the heart of a friend.

A Time to Talk

Robert Frost

When a friend calls to me from the road
And slows his horse to a meaning walk,
I don't stand still and look around
On all the hills I haven't hoed,
And shout from where I am, "What is it?"
No, not as there is a time to talk.
I thrust my hoe in the mellow ground,
Blade-end up and five feet tall,
And plod: I go up to the stone wall
For a friendly visit.

This breathtaking view of the North Fork White River at Flat Tops, Colorado, is inspiring evidence of the glories of the natural world. Photograph by Carr Clifton.

A Little Moment
Violet Bigelow Rourke

It takes a little moment
To send a line or two
To thank someone for
Doing something nice for you.
And soon that little moment
And the kind words that you say
Will be as golden hours
Of that someone's happy day.

Someone to Care
Ruby Lee Mitchell

Instead of pointing out the way,
I'd rather someone kind would say,
"I'll walk along with you, my friend;
The road has many turns and bends."

When life is dark and I can't see,
I'd rather one would say to me,
Instead of placing block or bar,
"Come on, I'll help you find a star."

If we'd share in life's give-and-take,
We must share with the friends we make.
With a friend, journeys seem less far;
With one to help, I touch a star.

For a Friend
Craig E. Sathoff

I believe in willows,
Simply for a willow's sake.
It does not fight the wind that blows;
It bends but does not break.

And I believe in friendship,
Simply for a friendship's sake.
It thrives in sunshine and in dark;
It learns to give and take.

I believe in willows,
For their branches move apart
To let the sunshine filter through
To warm a yearning heart.

The willow bears the weather well;
It bows before the wind.
But when the calm subdues the storm,
It stands with pride again.

I believe in friendship,
For, in life's fast-changing scene,
It bows before the cares of life
To rise strong, calm, and serene.

The soft colors of pansies and the blue of forget-me-nots combine for a lovely casual bouquet in PANSIES AND FORGET-ME-NOT, *a painting by Albert-Tibulle Furcy de LaVault. Image from Fine Art Photographic Library, Ltd., London/Julian Simon.*

HANDMADE HEIRLOOM

Melissa Lester

VICTORIAN CARDS

"The art of general letter-writing in the present day is shrinking until the letter threatens to become a telegram, a telephone message, a postcard," Emily Post lamented in 1922.

Young girls write to each other, no doubt, much as they did in olden times, and letters between young girls and young men flourish today like unpulled weeds in a garden where weeds were formerly never allowed to grow. It is the letter from the friend in this city to the friend in that, or from the traveling relative to the relative at home, that is gradually dwindling. As for the letter which younger relatives dutifully used to write—it has gone already with old-fashioned grace of speech and deportment.

If Post worried that communication was becoming abrupt and impersonal in her day, what would she think of today's world? Correspondence between friends is even more hurried in our age. However, time and technology cannot diminish the thrill of walking to the mailbox to find a letter handwritten by a friend.

As we sift through the pile of bills and solicitations, the familiar script of someone dear immediately brings a smile. There is an urge to tear open the envelope on the spot, yet we know this treasure is best opened in a special place. The

walk back from the mailbox is brisk; anticipation grows with each step. Once inside, all other mail is cast aside so that the letter may receive complete attention. Nestled in a favorite chair, we can at last open the envelope. We reread the letter several times so each word can be savored. And long after the rest of the day's mail has been discarded, the prized letter finds its place in a special box where it can be reopened whenever we wish to visit again.

As cherished as a handwritten letter is, correspondence from a friend is made all the more special when written on a hand-crafted card. The

---

I spent a delightful morning gathering several colors of pansies, carefully cutting the stems but leaving the calyxes.

---

tradition of making beautiful handmade cards can be traced to Victorian days. Richly embellished with silk, satin, lace, feathers, and even gold leaf, handmade cards became small works of art during this time. Pinprick and cutout designs created a lacy effect on some cards, and beautiful ribbons decorated others. Pictures of flowers, birds, and other lovely images were cut from paper called scrap art and layered with doilies and ribbons to create unique designs.

Eager to surprise a dear friend with a handmade Victorian card, I designed one with pressed pansies and ribbon. In Victorian times, flowers had a language all their own. Floral lexicons were published throughout the eighteenth century, allowing bouquets of flowers to communicate feelings of admiration, hope, or love. The pansy was said to represent thoughtful reflections, which made this flower the perfect choice for my card.

Feathers and scrap art combine to create a personalized card.
Photograph by Valentine Ward Evans/Mary Evans Picture Library/Alamy.

Pressing pansies is an enjoyable project. They should be gathered from the garden while still in prime condition. The best time is in the morning, after the dew has dried but before harsh sunlight causes them to wilt. I spent a delightful morning gathering several colors of pansies, carefully cutting the stems away but leaving the calyxes. I then placed the pansies between layers of tissue paper in an old phone book, not overlapping the petals. I set the phone book aside in a dry, out-of-the-way spot and stacked heavy books on top. After two weeks, the pansies were perfectly pressed and ready to decorate a handmade card.

An ecru, acid-free card provided a lovely background for the purple, yellow, and white pansies. Before gluing the pansies to the card, I gingerly laid out my design. Pressed pansies are delicate and should be handled carefully with fingers or tweezers. White glue thinned with water makes a decoupage medium. I lightly brushed the mixture onto the back of each pansy, then placed the pansies glue-side down on the note cards. With all the pansies in place, I lightly coated the front of each flower with the thinned glue. When the pansies dried, I used ribbon to complete the design. Then all that was left was to write my friend a letter and mail the card, hopeful that she would be touched by the reflection that went into each step of its creation.

In our hectic age, we need handwritten letters more than ever. Although technology allows us to communicate with ease and efficiency, our hearts still yearn for deeper connections. These bonds are often fortified through letters written from the heart. Even as she mourned the decline in letter writing in her day, Emily Post admitted, "Still, people do write letters in this day, and there are some who possess the divinely flexible gift for a fresh turn of phrase, for delightful keenness of observation." It is this possibility that makes us return to the mailbox each day, hopeful that inside we will find the reflections of a friend.

Melissa Lester is a freelance writer living in Wetumpka, Alabama, with her husband, two sons, and a new daughter. She contributes to a number of magazines and authored the book Giving for All It's Worth.

A Thank-You Note
Stella Craft Tremble

I think of cups of coffee that we poured
While thoughts and dreams our hearts explored,
An ideal world with Beauty as guide,
Who led where wishes were satisfied.
For all the varied themes we discussed,
I thank you, and for mutual love and trust.
For confidence that you bestowed,
For moments when our laughter flowed,
For thoughts of inspiration, truth, and art,
I cherish from the bottom of my heart.
For joys I took for granted, now I send
Appreciation and gratitude, my friend.

Appreciation
Edith Smuin Starke

Cherish that which you have today,
Lest circumstances take it away,
Leaving in its wake an empty place
And the touch of sorrow on your face.

Learn to master the art of living,
In both the taking and the giving;
And, when you give with all your heart,
In life's great plan, you've done your part.

Praise to Gentle Folk
Marion Doyle

God be thanked for gentle folk
Who know the art of kindliness,
Who go a step beyond their way
To aid another in distress,
However crowded be their day.

God be thanked for gentle folk
Who know the healing word to speak
When flesh recoils at pain's swift sting
Or hearts are galled by sorrow's yoke.
Kindness is a simple, blessed thing;
God smiles through the eyes of gentle folk.

*Fond reminiscences evoke thoughtful letters
at this writing table. Photograph by Jessie Walker.*

FAMILY RECIPES

Chewy Butterscotch Squares

Ann Buller, San Diego, California

½ cup evaporated milk	1 egg
½ cup chopped dates	¼ cup granulated sugar
½ cup golden raisins	1 3.4-ounce package butterscotch
½ cup butter	pudding mix
¼ cup confectioners' sugar	½ teaspoon baking powder
1 cup flour	1⅔ cups coconut

Preheat oven to 350°F. In a medium bowl, combine evaporated milk, dates, and raisins; set aside. In a large bowl, cream butter until light; mix in confectioners' sugar and flour. Pat into a greased, 8-by-8-inch pan. Bake 20 minutes. Remove from oven. In a large bowl, beat egg; stir in granulated sugar, pudding mix, baking powder, and coconut, mixing well. Gently stir in date mixture. Pour on top of baked crust. Bake 25 minutes. Makes 12 servings.

Raspberry Supreme Dessert

Dorothy Rieke, Julian, Nebraska

1½ cups flour, divided	2 eggs
1½ teaspoons baking powder	1 teaspoon vanilla
½ teaspoon salt	1 cup flake coconut
¼ cup butter	½ cup chopped pecans
1½ cups brown sugar, divided	1½ cups raspberries (rinsed and
2 teaspoons lemon juice	well-drained)

Preheat oven to 350°F. In a small bowl, sift 1¼ cups flour with baking powder and salt. Set aside. In a medium bowl, cream butter with ½ cup brown sugar until light. Stir in lemon juice. Set aside. Cut flour mixture into butter mixture until coarse crumbs form. Press into bottom of a greased, 9-by-9-inch pan. Bake 20 minutes or until lightly browned. Cool on a wire rack 5 minutes. In a medium bowl, whisk eggs, 1 cup brown sugar, ¼ cup flour, and vanilla. Stir in coconut and pecans. Spread raspberries evenly over crust; spread coconut mixture over raspberries. Return to oven and bake 30 minutes or until lightly browned. Cool in pan on wire rack. Makes 9 servings.

Brown Sugar Coconut Bars

Patricia Gojmerac, Rib Lake, Wisconsin

14 whole graham crackers	1 cup graham cracker crumbs
½ cup milk	1 8-ounce package cream cheese, softened
1 cup butter, divided	2 cups confectioners' sugar
1 cup brown sugar	1 teaspoon vanilla
1 cup coconut	

Line the bottom of a greased, 9-by-13-inch pan with whole graham crackers. In a large saucepan, heat milk and ½ cup butter, stirring until butter is melted. Stir in brown sugar, coconut, and graham cracker crumbs; boil until thickened, stirring occasionally, about 5 minutes. Pour mixture over graham crackers. Layer whole crackers over top. In a large bowl, cream together cream cheese, ½ cup butter, confectioners' sugar, and vanilla. Spread over top of bars. Cool. Cut into squares. Makes 12 squares.

Butterscotch Banana Squares

Joan Nesmith, Williams, Minnesota

1½ cups flour	1 cup brown sugar, packed
¼ teaspoon cinnamon	2 eggs, beaten
½ teaspoon baking powder	½ teaspoon vanilla
½ teaspoon baking soda	2 ripe bananas, mashed
½ teaspoon salt	1 cup butterscotch chips
½ cup butter, softened	

Preheat oven to 350°F. In a medium bowl, sift together flour, cinnamon, baking powder, baking soda, and salt. Set aside. In a large bowl, cream butter with brown sugar. Add eggs, vanilla, and banana; mix well. Add dry ingredients to butter mixture, mixing thoroughly. Spread evenly in a greased, 9-by-9-inch pan. Sprinkle with butterscotch chips. Bake 30 minutes. Makes 9 servings.

Wrapped in pretty gift boxes, these treats offer a sweet reminder for your friends of your love and care. Gifts from the kitchen are special gifts from the heart. We would love to try your favorite recipe too. Send a typed copy to Ideals Publications, 535 Metroplex Drive, Suite 250, Nashville, Tennessee 37211. Payment will be provided for each recipe published.

The Friendship Quilt

Rita B. Hollingworth

It's an old family keepsake, made long ago.
A woman in those days had time to sew.
She patiently pieced it, patch beside patch,
With initials embroidered in colors to match,
And it always intrigues me, there on the bed,
All hand-feather-stitched with bright-colored thread.
"This piece of white satin with initials of white
Was worn by your mother on her wedding night;
This piece of velvet, so rich and so red,
Was worn once by your grandma," she said.
A patch of blue taffeta Aunt Lou had worn;
A bow from the bonnet Grace wore Easter morn;
A scrap of gray necktie marked H. W. D.
(He was the fellow who jilted Aunt Bea);
Each set of initials an old memory brings
Of joy or unhappy, personal things.
Long bygone days filled with pleasure and woe
Are traced in this friendship quilt made long ago.

When people are true
friends, even shared
water tastes sweet.
—CHINESE PROVERB

Fresh lemonade and comfortable quilts offer a relaxing afternoon respite.
Photograph by Dianne Dietrich Leis/Dietrich Leis Stock Photography.

The Quilted Life
Elaine B. Porter

How like a patchwork quilt life seems—
Bits of reality, pieces of dreams,
Fastened together, vivid and muted,
Fabric and colors to each moment suited.
Feathered stitches of friendship and love
Hold fast through good times and bad.
Those tiny, blessed stitches from above
Keep us warm in good weather or bad,
Give us reasons to be happy and glad.

Granny's Quilts
Mildred L. Jarrell

Little scraps of colored calico,
All cut into squares,
Then mixed and matched,
And sewed in row on row;
Reds and greens and polka dots,
Striped squares and then plain,
Little blue forget-me-nots,
And yellow daisy chain—

Tiny stitches laid so neat
Held them all together,
As Granny pieced and sewed her quilts,
All during winter weather.
Soon the frame was set up,
A joyous time for me,
When neighbor ladies visited,
And sewed, then later stayed for tea.

Each finished quilt she scented
With petals she had dried,
Now ready to give away
With a note of love inside.
Although the years have slipped away,
I treasure the fond memory
Of the dearest Granny ever
And the quilts she made for me.

*A shaded porch is the perfect spot for a lazy summer
afternoon. Photograph by Dianne Dietrich
Leis/Dietrich Leis Stock Photography.*

REMEMBER WHEN

Jackie Paschall

PURRING ENGINES AND SUNDAY DRIVES

Some of the sweetest memories can be triggered by the most unlikely chores. I was helping a friend put up wallpaper when the aroma of the paper soaking in the tray of warm water brought back memories of my grandfather's starched shirts. Closing my eyes, I could almost hear the squeak of the screen door which preceded the loud bang announcing my after-school arrival at my grandparents' house, next door to my own. I felt blessed to have my best friends, my grandparents, living next door.

After supper at my grandparents' home, the crickets and whippoorwills would call us to the front porch swing to escape the heat of the kitchen stove. My grandmother would join us after the dishes were washed. Wearing her customary housedress and apron, she would sit with her large arms folded across her generous midriff and her eyes closed behind bifocal glasses. There was always a long strand of stray hair that needed coaxing back to the tightly braided, graying wreath that framed her wide face. She would critique my grandfather's "tall tales," as she liked to call them, without opening her eyes.

On pleasant evenings the neighborhood was busy with people strolling or driving by. Few of the cars on the street had air conditioning and many didn't have turn signals, so a turn was announced with an arm hung out the driver's window. A friendly wave and a hello were as automatic as an upturned right signal. Grandfather greeted everyone by name.

Not only did he know everyone by name, but he could tell what kind of car was coming down the street behind him without even turning around. Selling cars was his business, and he boasted that he could identify any car by the

---

With a white-gloved hand, Grandmother held tightly to her straw hat.

---

sound of its engine. The Chryslers had the powerful Firepower engines. Fords, some of the fastest and most affordable cars of the time, had that Fordomatic drive with no clutch and a powerful V-8 engine. They could take off like a bullet from a standstill. By 1955, most younger men on the street were following Detroit's advice to "see the USA in your Chevrolet." The roar of the small block V-8 engines could be heard about as frequently as the sound of Elvis on the radio. But my favorite car was the Chevrolet Bel Air Sport Sedan, with its two-toned paint job and white-walled tires. The very distinctive 88 Oldsmobile, which came out in the early 1950s with its brand-new, gas-saving rocket engine and Body by Fisher, was the easiest to identify.

I discovered later that Grandfather had sold most of the cars that he was identifying by sound and knew the approximate time the drivers arrived home in the evening. It was an impressive feat, nonetheless.

My grandmother loved riding on Sunday afternoons listening to Grandfather's recollections of old customers and the places he had visited them to make a sale. Dressed in his whitest dress shirt with sleeves rolled up, dark suspenders fastened to his trousers, and a black felt dress hat with a wide brim, Grandfather would help her into the passenger side. With a white-gloved hand, Grandmother held tightly to her straw hat, adorned with a colorful bunch of fruit and a wisp of a veil brushing her cheekbones; she clutched her handbag in the other hand. She was usually dressed in a fine-looking, lace-collared frock sewn for her by her sister.

Neighbors wave as they pass by on a Sunday drive. Photograph from Retrofile/Roberstock.

I would wait impatiently in the back seat with the windows already rolled down. My grandparents drove a different used car every week, but most of them had running boards, wide mohair-covered bench seats, wool carpeting, plenty of headroom, and space to stretch your legs.

The wide bumpers and shiny hood ornament glistened in the sun as we would pass under arches of leafy shade trees, leaving behind clouds of dust which hung in the air like puffs of smoke. I could ride for hours listening to the sound of my grandfather's voice, interrupted by the occasional draw on his pipe and my grandmother's laughter, which started softly and ended with tears in her eyes. The afternoon drive would come to a crunchy stop on loose gravel when the perfect shady spot was spotted along some one-lane road.

With a turn of the key, Grandfather would open the trunk to reveal a juicy, cold watermelon resting on a bed of newspapers. After sectioning the watermelon, he would use his pocket knife to dig out a hole in the dust on the side of the road for a game of silver dollars. The technique of spinning a large silver dollar with a flick of the wrist so it landed square in the hole was carefully explained to me at the onset of each and every throw.

After the last piece of watermelon was eaten, I would reluctantly climb back into the car with sticky, dusty fingers, and by sunset we would arrive home. Hats were returned to their hatboxes, and Sunday clothes were hung back in the mirrored chifforobe.

That old black felt hat that Grandfather wore and a few of the silver dollars we used to throw are tucked away in my home. Today they bring back memories as sweet as a cold watermelon on a hot day. And on warm evenings, I still enjoy the game of identifying the make of a neighbor's car simply by the sound of its engine.

Jackie Paschall is a pastor's wife and former grade school teacher who loves to share family stories with her grandchildren on her back porch in Paris, Tennessee.

Great Art of Kindness

June Masters Bacher

I shall hope my heart soon finds
A garden path that winds and winds
Among bright flowers of all creeds
That seem to know each other's needs,
That nod and bloom with naught in mind
But that great art of being kind.

Insomuch as anyone pushes you nearer to God, he or she is your friend.
—Author Unknown

Valued Deeds

Roy Z. Kemp

A little, cheerful, friendly smile
That eases painful heart
May be remembered many times,
Long after you depart.

A small act of decency,
A deed to show respect,
May be the greatest ever done,
For great is its effect.

A little word of friendliness
By which a heart is fed
May be the most important word
That you have ever said.

These deep purple clematis blossoms make gettting the mail a special event. Photograph by Nancy Matthews.

I Love My Friend

Joan Teague

She trusts me with her secret dreams,
Hidden thoughts and not-so-noble schemes,
Silent sorrow of wounds not healed,
Small triumphs that when revealed
Become much larger than they were.
So many things I have seen in her,
Things within myself I thought unfit
And so denied, but sharing frees me to admit.
Her gift of self makes me the debtor;
Loving her, I love myself a little better.

My Truest Friend

Georgia B. Adams

Each time that I have thoughts of you,
It causes me to smile,
For you have done so very much
To make my life worthwhile.

You've been on hand when came my way
A test or trial sore;
You've wept with me, you've prayed with me,
And, what is even more,

You've actually made all my life
Your very chief concern;
And, as the highway of this life
Makes here and there a turn,

You've been at every crossroad
With a helping hand to lend.
That's why I'll always treasure you,
My best, my truest friend.

The Leftover Smile

Keith W. Johnson

She smiled engagingly to greet
A casual friend she chanced to meet.
As she continued on her way,
The smile did momentarily stay
To prompt an unknown passerby
With warmth to beamingly reply
With a smile that also tarried,
Until it too had been carried
Unto a person that he met,
Who passed it to another yet.

And so the smile went up the street;
It passed both ways with each repeat,
Till scarcely anywhere in town
Was found a grimace or a frown.

Tea and roses and a warm breeze present a lovely setting for a friendly conversation. Photograph by Nancy Matthews.

Friendships
Amelia Evans Mix

Of all the gifts we are given on earth,
Friends are of the greatest worth.
Some friends have interests like our own,
But, when dark trouble comes,
Best friends are then made known.
While we give friendship to sad, lonely souls,
Another may aid and further our goals.
A friend knows our deepest needs,
Before we know ourselves,
And intercedes.

One More Thing
Donna Miesbach

If I could
I'd give you
Wings to fly your special skies,
And courage, too,
I'd send to you
To help your spirits rise.
And breezes fair
And swaying trees,
And lovely star-filled nights—
I'd like to give you
All of these
To make your days just right.

And then I'd do
Just one thing more:
A prayer of praise I'd send
Because I feel
So very blessed
To have you for my friend.

*Black-eyed Susans add bold color to the harbor at
Sister Bay, Wisconsin, along the Green Bay shoreline.
Photograph by Ken Dequaine Photography.*

39

A Wish

Lorine Lile

Give me a friend to walk with me,
A friend who loves me well,
Who understands the silent needs
My lips may never tell,
Whose heart bears answer to my heart,
Whose strength is mine to borrow,
Whose love and faith are knit with mine,
And I'll not fear the morrow.

Give me a friend to stand by me
In hours of darkest pain,
Who is acquainted with my faults,
Yet bears no word of blame;
A friend whose laughter echoes mine
Until my days are spent,
Whose tears are mingled with my own;
And I shall be content.

Give me a friend to walk with me,
A friend whose heart has known
The silent depths in which the soul
Must sometimes strive alone,
A friend who counsels wisely
And rebukes, if I have need.
If I have one such friend as this,
I shall be rich indeed.

A Friend

Author Unknown

I will not think that I have failed,
Or lived my life in vain,
If to my credit I shall find
One friend to be my gain;
And, though the road of life is rough
With mountains hard to climb,
I find there's joy along the way,
And the journey, it is fine,
If there is a friend beside me
To cheer me with his song,
To smile his understanding
When everything goes wrong.
It gives me strength and courage
The mountains to ascend,
And I find that life's worth living
As long as there's a friend.
Then be not hasty when I'm gone
To say I lived in vain,
Though ghosts of many failures
Like monuments remain.
But when life's sun is sinking
And I reach my journey's end,
Then count my earthly riches
In the number of my friends.

These starfish and seashells, natural ornaments of the shore,
would delight any collector walking along the beach.
Photograph by William H. Johnson.

Recipe for Friendship

Nancy Haynes

Equal parts of kindness,
Unselfishness, and caring;
Mix with love, respect, and trust,
And add some secret-sharing.
Sprinkle some laughter and helping words;
Scatter some dreams and pleasure.
How much do you add of each of these?
In friendship there's too much to measure.

Flower of Friendship

Anne Campbell

Our friendship needs no special care
To keep its rose in bloom.
Its fragrance lingers everywhere,
In sunshine or in gloom.

Like the perennials that lift
Their blossoms to the sun,
It will survive, this precious gift,
When summer days are done.

The winter of my life draws near,
But happily I know
The friendship that I hold so dear
Will bloom beneath the snow.

On Friendship

Judith Nelson

To know that should I choose to speak,
In patience you will hear,
Or, if in sorrow I must weep,
You're there to share my tear.
When laughter fills my heart and soul,
My joy belongs to you;
And should I wish to reminisce,
You'll walk that pathway too.
If fear surrounds as deepest night,
Your hand assurance gives.
And though I err or miss a step,
Your faith in me still lives.

My one desire above all else
Is very much a cherished wish:
To know and then to try to be
The kind of friend you are to me.

*The magnificent blues and greens of the
Atlantic Ocean at Block Island,
Rhode Island, capture the eye.
Photograph by William H. Johnson.*

43

READERS' REFLECTIONS

Readers are invited to submit original poetry for possible publication in future issues of IDEALS. *Please send typed copies only; manuscripts will not be returned. Writers receive payment for each published submission. Send material to Readers' Reflections, Ideals Publications, 535 Metroplex Drive, Suite 250, Nashville, Tennessee 37211.*

End of Summer
Fran Echler, Toledo, Ohio

I almost missed the end of summer,
Fretting of things not important at all.
Quietly it had slipped away;
Before I realized, it had turned to fall.

I almost missed the end of summer—
The steady hum of the locusts' song,
Hard green crab apples turning red,
Evening shadows growing long.

I almost missed the end of summer—
Hot, humid days that end in rain;
Ripe, juicy tomatoes from a neighbor,
Homegrown, just eaten plain.

I almost missed the end of summer—
Goldfinches perched on tall sunflowers.
How could I not notice the clash of seasons,
End-of-summer storms, their awesome power?

Vacation at the Lake
Ethel Worm, Cologne, Minnesota

It's midnight, and, after a long day's ride, everyone is fast asleep. I am alone, sitting by the window with my elbows on the windowsill, holding up my cheeks. All at once I see a most beautiful sight: a gentle breeze is making little waves, and on the tip of each wave is a little light. I wonder if it might be fireflies out playing in the night, when I look up and see the sky is filled with millions of stars. It seems like they are sliding down the Milky Way and then landing on the tip of each wave, then tumbling into the lake for a midnight swim. This night I'll always treasure, engrave on my mind forever, this reflection of a star-filled sky putting on a water ballet just for me.

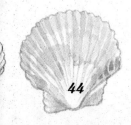

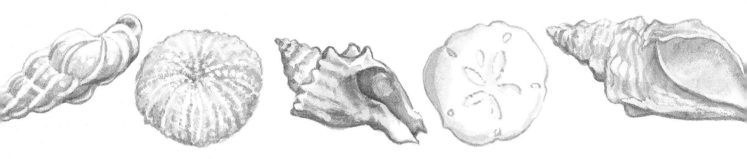

Found: A Treasure on the Beach
Roberta Carpenter, Goshen, Indiana

A treasure map I found,
Written on the sand,
Leading me to who knows where,
Perhaps another land.

I followed tiny footprints
Three paces to the right
And came upon a crawdad,
Who tried to take a bite.

Five paces on, a sharp turn left,
And then I saw, with glee,
Some driftwood, bleached and gnarled,
Just waiting there for me.

With map as guide, I traveled where
Each tiny track would lead
And found some shiny seashells
Among the green seaweed.

At last I solved the mystery
Written in the sand;
It was just a busy sandpiper,
Making tracks upon the land.

Walk on a Cape Cod Beach
Lorraine E. Mitchell, Hatboro, Pennsylvania

Today I was a millionaire
And walked my vast domain.
I paced along its rolling edge
And watched it wax and wane;
I glimpsed the canopy of blue
With white ships set a-sail.
I heard the cries of flying gulls
That wheeled and then turned tail,
When finding on their spot of land
My person there alone;
With graceful sweep and plaintive cry,
They wished that I'd be gone.

But I became a millionaire
And owned that stretch of sand;
I plucked my wealth and held it,
Glistening, in my hand.
The dunes were mine, the floating clouds
In blue sky, out of reach,
The water spreading lacy frills
All up and down the beach.
My wealth was sight and sound
Of changing, changeless sea
And shore dunes stretching endlessly
In glorious panoply.

Lights of Love
Laura Wittman Pegg, Santa Clara, Utah

Within the deep and sleepy night,
The coyotes bay up at the sight
Of starlit skies displayed above
And crystal balls that hang in love.

They gaze upon the earth below,
With brilliant streams of light to sow
In every fragile human's heart;
Their gifts become a work of art.

Overleaf: The Grand Tetons are reflected in a beaver pond near Schwabacher Landing on the Snake River in the Grand Teton National Park, Wyoming. Photograph by Terry Donnelly/Donnelly Austin Photography.

45

THROUGH MY WINDOW

Pamela Kennedy

ON THE ROAD WITH MOM

My mother and I have always been best friends. And we have always enjoyed traveling together. Our trips have changed in character over the years, but our enjoyment of them never seems to wane.

The earliest trip I recall was when I was "four, going on five." I specifically remember my age because I told everyone repeatedly on the Shasta Daylight train all the way from Seattle to Sacramento. The other thing I did repeatedly was get train-sick. My mother booked a sleeping car, thinking that if I were asleep part of the trip I'd be less likely to become ill. Her plan didn't work. But I enjoyed the trip anyway and still remember sitting in the glass-domed car watching the towns and fields pass by.

After my performance on the train, we concentrated on car trips—short ones. Traveling from Kent to Seattle was a real outing, even though it only covered about twenty miles. I remember being amazed by my mother's ability to find her way through the highways and city streets and end up exactly where she wanted to be. I had no idea how she did it! Sometimes we shopped or toured a museum or art gallery, but we always ended up at the Times Tea Room, where I was allowed to order from the menu myself and even count out the cash to pay our bill.

The summer I was fifteen, having overcome my carsickness, Mother and I traveled from Washington state to Missouri to visit her sister's family. We started early each morning and stopped as often as we liked at fresh fruit stands and antique shops. By the time we arrived at my uncle's farm, we had a carnival-glass cake plate, a couple of cut-glass wine goblets, and a little maple rocker in the trunk of the old Dodge. On the trip back, we sat at

---

Mother said, "Now this is an interesting adventure we hadn't planned."

---

the counter in a little diner one morning and struck up a conversation with a fellow who wondered about our travels.

"You two ladies travelin' by yerselves?" he asked.

"Yes, we are," Mother replied. "And we plan to make it to Omaha by tonight."

"Can't be done by a woman driver," the fellow countered. "That's nearly four hundred miles and it's already eight in the morning."

We drove six hundred miles that day and I'm still convinced Mother did it just to spite that man at the diner!

After I was married, the Navy took my husband to sea on several six- to eight-month deployments. Early on, when we were on a tight budget and without children, I always returned home during his absences. This led to half a dozen trips with Mom, either north or south along the West

Coast. I remember those long trips driving the "grapevine" on Interstate 5. We traded off driving every two hours and talked about everything under the sun. The time went by quickly and, lulled by our conversations, we did not notice the miles slip away and the speedometer climb. I recall one long afternoon when I glanced up from the book I was reading to look at the dashboard. My usually conservative mother was humming along at ninety miles an hour!

After my father passed away, Mother and I decided to take a couple of international trips. The first was to Hong Kong, where we used just about every mode of transportation available. We hopped on city buses, climbed down into the subway, took the Star Ferry across the harbor, and rode the tram straight up Victoria Peak. We did our Christmas shopping in an open-air market and even took in some unexpected local culture when Mother's wallet was stolen by a pickpocket and we had to make a police report. We also experienced a day at the American Embassy replacing her passport. I would have expected her, at seventy-five, to be more unnerved by the experience, but, in her typical style, as we worked our way through the crowds outside the embassy, Mother said, "Now this is an interesting adventure we hadn't planned!"

Two years later we went to England and spent a couple of wonderful weeks visiting historical sites, attending plays, and visiting charming bed-and-breakfast establishments from Canterbury to Bath. In London, we resided at a hotel where the "Lake Country Brewery Owners Football Fans" were stay-

ing during the national playoffs. One evening, as we traversed the lobby, Mother was propositioned by a couple of inebriated soccer fans, feeling frisky after an afternoon of cheering their team to victory. She handled it beautifully with a smile and a wave, "Not tonight, fellows, we're due at the theater!"

My mother now resides in a retirement community, and I live 2,500 miles away, but we are still planning another trip. We're driving to Vancouver, British Columbia, to stay in a Victorian bed-and-breakfast and take in some of the local gardens and parks. If it proves to be like our other mother-daughter excursions, it will be jam-packed with wonderful conversation, great memories, and at least a few unexpected adventures!

Pamela Kennedy is a freelance writer of short stories, articles, essays, and children's books. Wife of a retired naval officer and mother of three children, she has made her home on both U.S. coasts and currently resides in Honolulu, Hawaii.

Original artwork by Meredith Johnson.

To a Friend Starting on a Journey

Grace V. Watkins

I wish you mountains green and tall,
A silver gleaming waterfall.
I wish you the ocean's blue delight
And myriad stars within the night,
Valleys of flowers so bright and fair,
They seem a shining prelude to prayer.
But however wondrous the things you see,
I wish your coming home may be
A heart-stirring thrill, a joy more deep
Than any ocean or valley's sweep.

The Ribbon Road

Robert Freeman Bound

My song is in the wind
As it sweeps the sea
And the hills that border the shore.
When a wanderer's moon
Lights summer fields,
I know I must leave once more.

Then my heart insists,
As it always will,
That I trek the ribbon road,
Which leads to new friends everywhere
And starts by my abode.

In the Train

James Thomson

As we rush, as we rush in the train,
The trees and the houses go wheeling back,
But the starry heavens above the plain
Come flying on our track.

All the beautiful stars of the sky,
The silver doves of the forest of night,
Over the dull earth swarm and fly,
Companions of our flight.

We will rush ever on without fear;
Let the goal be far, the flight be fleet!
For we carry the heavens with us, dear,
While the earth slips from our feet!

Moonrise in the Rockies

Ella Higginson

The trembling train clings to the leaning wall
Of solid stone; a thousand feet below
Sinks a black gulf; the sky hangs like a pall
Upon the peaks of everlasting snow.
Then suddenly springs a rim of light,
Curved like a silver sickle. High and higher,
Till the full moon burns on the breast of night,
And a million firs stand tipped with lucent fire.

An old-fashioned steam engine chugs through the Rocky Mountains near Chama, New Mexico. Photograph by H. Armstrong Roberts.

TRAVELER'S DIARY

D. Fran Morley

GOLDEN SPIKE NATIONAL HISTORIC SITE
PROMONTORY SUMMIT, UTAH

The desert north of the Great Salt Lake in Utah is a sparsely occupied land, but on a spring day in 1869, Promontory Summit might as well have been the center of the universe. For years, thousands of men had worked day and night and endured unimaginable hardships in an effort to reach this seemingly insignificant spot in the vast American West. On May 10, 1869, during a ceremony noted around the world through the medium of telegraph, officials hammered in the final spikes that made the Union Pacific and Central Pacific railroads one continuous line. For the first time in history, a physical link stretched across the great American frontier.

The stories that came out of the building of the transcontinental railroad are some of the most fascinating from America's history. Larger-than-life individuals made their reputations and staked massive fortunes on a scheme that succeeded thanks to the labor of America's immigrants, including thousands of new arrivals from China and Ireland. I was eager to learn more about this time, so on a trip though the West a few years ago, my husband and I visited the Golden Spike National Historic Site.

HISTORY OF THE SITE

One of the first things I learned is that nothing at the site is original to 1869. In 1903, the railroad built a bridge across Great Salt Lake and the famous stretch of tracks at Promontory Summit became just a local line for farmers and ranchers; then, in 1942, the government tore up the all-but-abandoned tracks for the war effort. Area residents began holding memorial reenactments of the driving of the last spike a few years after World War II ended, and, in 1957, Congress authorized the creation of the Golden Spike National Historic Site.

Today, the historic site encompasses 2,176 acres, which includes a two-mile stretch of track, with switches and side lines, replicas of the two

---

Despite the name, the ceremony actually included four honorary spikes.

---

telegraph lines that broadcast the news in 1869; a visitor's center and bookstore; plus walking and driving trails. I was pleased to see full-size replicas of the two steam engines, the Union Pacific's *No. 119* and the Central Pacific's *Jupiter*, and surprised to learn that when these two engines made their reenactment debut in 1980, they were the first steam engines built in the U.S. in twenty-five years.

At the Visitor's Center, we spent time looking at photos and reading about the incredible effort it took to build the railroads. At the display about the 1869 Golden Spike ceremony, I learned that, despite the name, the ceremony actually included four honorary spikes. A San Francisco construction magnate donated the famous golden spike that carried the names of the directors of the Central Pacific Railroad, a San Francisco newspaper contributed a second golden spike, officials from Nevada supplied a silver spike, and a spike that was a blend of iron, silver, and gold represented Arizona. All of the ceremonial spikes were dropped into holes in a pre-drilled laurelwood tie and gently tapped into place.

Unfortunately, the Visitor's Center displays only a replica of the first golden spike. The original golden spike, Nevada's silver spike, and Arizona's spike are on exhibit at various locations around the country. No one knows for certain what happened to the second gold spike.

CEREMONIAL REENACTMENT

Our visit was on a summer weekend, so we were fortunate to catch several of the demonstrations and reenactments that local volunteers put on during the park's busy season. With other visitors, we hurried outside to watch as the two massive steam engines chugged and puffed their way toward each other. A ranger pointed out that the Union Pacific's *No. 119* was powered by coal while the Central Pacific's *Jupiter* ran on wood. The ranger explained that one engine came across the plains, which were devoid of trees, and the other came through the mountains, which meant that wood fuel was plentiful.

As the two steam giants neared each other, costumed actors picked up hammers and recreated the auspicious Golden Spike ceremony. And, just as in 1869, after the officials had completed their speeches, two nearly anonymous workers hammered in the ordinary iron spike that actually joined the two rail lines.

BIG FILL WALK

Before leaving the park, we hiked the short Big Fill Walk to get an idea about what working conditions were like for the railroad crews in the 1860s, then drove a nine-mile, self-guided auto tour that runs along the historic old railroad grade. Later, as we continued on our trip, we talked about how train travel changed the West, reducing the journey across the continent from six months to about a week. It was truly, as we had learned, the beginning of the end for the great American frontier.

When not gallivanting around the country, travel writer Fran Morley spends time with her husband, Tom, and their cat, Gracie, in beautiful Fairhope, Alabama.

Replicas of the Union Pacific's No. 119 *and the Central Pacific's* JUPITER *help re-create a significant achievement in United States history. Photograph courtesy of Golden Spike National Historic Site.*

My Hope
Bert Whitehouse

This I believe and this my creed:
That ere my journey ends,
I'll earn the love, and joy it brings,
Of just a few good friends.

This I believe and this my creed:
I'll share with him—my friend—
My heart, my prayers, his load, his cares
Until my journey ends.

Hometown
Marie Fouts

It is just a small town
Where hopes and dreams come true,
Just a small, quiet town,
With friendship running
    through and through.

Some streets have lovely old houses
Lined with trees on either side,
And rolling lawns and gardens
Are a source of pride.

There are schools and several churches,
With a few shops here and there,
And the large and stately courthouse
That overlooks the square.

We can see the wide and lazy river
Running along the edge of town,
With families picnicking or fishing
And children running all around.

No wonder, when I travel far,
For this dear town I yearn;
Though larger cities beckon me,
It is here I will return—

Where there is no need to hurry,
And the air is calm and clear—
To this quiet little town,
Where every friend is dear.

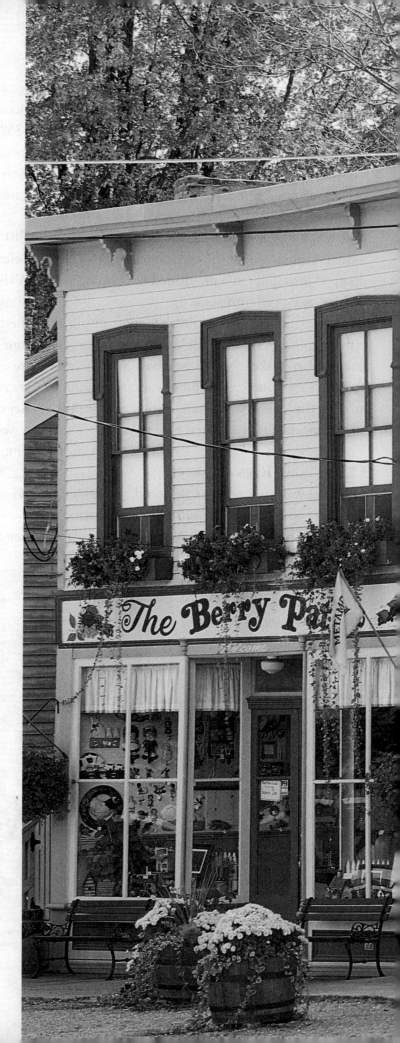

The attractive storefronts invite visitors to browse in Metamora, Indiana. Photograph by Daniel Dempster.

WHEN WE THINK OF FRIENDS, AND CALL THEIR FACES OUT OF THE SHADOWS, AND THEIR VOICES OUT OF THE ECHOES THAT FAINT ALONG THE CORRIDORS OF MEMORY, AND DO IT WITHOUT KNOWING WHY SAVE THAT WE LOVE TO DO IT, WE CONTENT OURSELVES THAT THAT FRIENDSHIP IS A REALITY, AND NOT A FANCY— THAT IT IS BUILT UPON A ROCK, AND NOT UPON THE SANDS THAT DISSOLVE AWAY WITH THE EBBING TIDES AND CARRY THEIR MONUMENTS WITH THEM.

—MARK TWAIN

ENDURING FRIENDS

Gertrude Rudberg

New friendships come, old friendships go;
But those remaining seem to grow
Because they're built throughout the years
On understanding, joy, and tears.

All friendships should be kept a prize
Because within, a kinship cries
For fellowship and human love
That's sent to all from God above.

Real friendships are so rare, we know;
They fizzle, burn, and then flame low,
Often lost in ash of anger and pain,
A spark once there dies out in vain.

Some friendships last, some fade away,
But friends worthwhile will always stay
Faithful, trusting, forgiving too,
Always loyal, always true.

OLD FRIENDSHIPS

June Masters Bacher

Old friendships last forever,
Forever and a day;
Like pictures in an album,
The hearts and faces stay.

Old friendships are unchanging;
They're ever fresh and sweet;
They wait at intersections
Where past and present meet.

Old friendships grow more precious
With each passing year;
They've learned to share life's laughter
And let it dry each tear.

Old friends are the treasure
Kept always bright and new
By saying to each other,
"The way we used to do."

Old friendships last forever;
The hearts and faces stay,
Like pictures in an album,
Forever and a day.

This sunny porch is the perfect setting for a cheerful breakfast. Photograph by Jessie Walker.

57

COLLECTOR'S CORNER

Melinda Rathjen

VINTAGE LUGGAGE

As I was packing for a short trip last week, I came across an old suitcase in the back of my closet. The small, pink leather suitcase reminded me of the summer I was eight years old and my grandmother drove my cousin Amy, my sister Angela, and me from southern Illinois to Kirkwood, Missouri, to visit our great-aunt Saralee and great-uncle Elmer. We three girls carried our pink suitcases, identical except for our initials embroidered on the lid. Even stuffed with souvenirs from a St. Louis adventure, my suitcase was light enough for me to carry by myself, and I did so proudly.

Luggage has not always been so portable. The sizes, shapes, materials, and construction of luggage have evolved along with the modes of transportation. The history of luggage is essentially the history of transportation.

In the early 1800s, a family's possessions often had to fit into one or two trunks for travel by ship or horse-drawn wagon. The trunks were very large, with handles on each end, and required at least two people to carry them. Wardrobe trunks, first seen in the 1870s, stood on one end and allowed easy access to both hanging clothes and storage drawers. It was then common for a traveler to take his or her entire wardrobe along on a trip.

The railroads helped increase the ease and frequency of travel; and as a result, the choices available in sizes and shapes of luggage increased. As the average trip length decreased, the traveler needed to pack less and thus the dimensions of the luggage were reduced. In 1903, the French luggage company Louis Vuitton introduced the Ideal Trunk, designed to hold just one week's travel necessities.

Half of American families owned a car by 1930, and luggage companies began catering to the distinct demands of travel by automobile. The luggage needed to be smaller and lighter to enable easy loading for spur-of-the-moment trips. As early as 1897, some companies worked directly with automobile manufacturers to design suitcases and exterior trunks (which later became a standard feature) that fit specific automobile models.

When commercial air travel began to take off, concerns about weight limits on the flying machines caused new trends in luggage production. Made of wicker, vulcanized fiber, raffia, or lightweight metal, the cases for travel by air were by necessity smaller and lighter than those for automobile travel. In 1924, Louis Vuitton introduced the Keepall, a revolutionary soft-sided bag that popularized the duffel bag shape and the concept of frameless luggage.

Luggage is emblematic of wide open spaces and new experiences. My pink suitcase, waiting in my closet, reminds me of my childhood travels and of the possibilities that are packed into the future, just a suitcase away.

CARRY ON THE TRADITION OF VINTAGE LUGGAGE

When shopping for vintage luggage, consider the following:

GETTING STARTED:

•Search for vintage luggage at antique stores, estate sales, auctions, flea markets, and even thrift stores.

•Check the condition of any stitching, leather, interior materials, hinges, handles, latches, and locks.

•Limit your collection by shape or intended use. Consider hatboxes, suitcases, portmanteaus, valises, wardrobe trunks, kit or doctor's bags, for example.

CASES:

•Exterior materials include: canvas, leather (made from the skins of cows, crocodiles, and even ostriches), wicker, and metal.

•Pieces may be hinged and/or stitched together; some may have protective corner caps or edging made of leather, metal, or canvas.

•The types of handles and locks vary and may be helpful in determining the age and value of the piece.

INTERIOR:

•Luggage was often lined with silk, linen, canvas, velvet, or leather.

•Women's blouse cases and men's dressing kits included items such as hairbrushes, mirrors, and various bottles kept in pockets on the interior.

LABELS AND MARKS:

•Look for a manufacturer or retail label, which usually appears inside the case or on the exterior near the handle.

•If you can locate the original owner's name or intials, or destination or hotel labels, these provide interesting insight into the traveling history of the

Vintage luggage has become another appealing way of providing individual touches to home décor. Photograph by Jessie Walker.

luggage. Beware of faux destination labels, which unscrupulous dealers may add for aesthetic appeal.

•Well-known manufacturers/retailers include:

Hermés (est. 1837, France)
Drew & Sons Ltd. (est. 1844, England)
Louis Vuitton (est. 1854, France)
Hartmann Trunk Company (est. 1877, USA)
Globe-Trotter (est. 1897, USA)
Samsonite (est. 1910, USA)

BAGGAGE HANDLING:

•Protect the exterior of your vintage luggage with leather protectant or an exterior cloth or canvas cover.

•Display your collection creatively, for example, as coffee or side tables or even blanket chests.

Melinda Rathjen, when not traveling to Illinois to visit family, makes her home in Nashville, Tennessee, with her sister and two mischievous cats.

BITS & PIECES

With reason one can travel the world over;
without it, it is hard to move an inch.
—*Chinese Proverb*

Blessed is the man that beholdeth the face
of a friend in a far country.
—*Henry van Dyke*

To travel hopefully is a better
thing than to arrive.
—*Robert Louis Stevenson*

The whole object of travel is not to set foot
on foreign land; it is at last to set foot on one's
own country as a foreign land.
—*G. K. Chesterton*

At your return, visit our house; let old
acquaintance be renewed.
—*William Shakespeare*

I never travel without my diary. One should always
have something sensational to read in the train.
—*Oscar Wilde*

A journey of a thousand miles
starts from beneath one's feet.
—*Lao-Tzu*

*T*o finish the moment, to find the journey's end
in every step of the road, to live the greatest
number of good hours, is wisdom.

—*Ralph Waldo Emerson*

*L*et me recommend the best medicine in the
world: a long journey, at a mild season, through
a pleasant country, in easy stages.

—*James Madison*

*O*ne never reaches home, but wherever friendly paths
intersect, the whole world looks like home for a time.

—*Herman Hesse*

*O*ne can never read all the books in the world,
nor travel all its roads.

—*Author Unknown*

LEGENDARY AMERICANS

Maud Dawson

GRENVILLE MELLEN DODGE

On May 10, 1869, the United States celebrated as a united country what at the time was called the Eighth Wonder of the World. In Chicago, the biggest parade of the century began; in Philadelphia, the Liberty Bell was rung; in San Francisco, 220 cannons heralded the city; more than seven thousand people crowded the Tabernacle in Salt Lake City, and in other cities throughout the United States people blew whistles, lit firecrackers, gave speeches, and sang praises in churches. The country, so lately torn by the Civil War, was reuniting in recognition of the completion of the major engineering feat of the nineteenth century—the transcontinental railroad. One Congressional commission at the time reported, "In the grandeur and magnitude of the undertaking, it has never been equaled."

Many people were involved in this project that connected the East with the West; however, only one man was credited then and now with being "the man that built the railroad"—Grenville Dodge, of Council Bluffs, Iowa. The Chief Engineer for the Union Pacific, which built more than one thousand miles of the approximate total of seventeen hundred miles of track, he was a Civil War hero and an experienced surveyor. Both President Abraham Lincoln and President Ulysses S. Grant respected and admired the younger general. General William T. Sherman notified the board of directors of the Union Pacific that Dodge should be hired and encouraged him to leave the Army and accept the position in 1866.

The obstacles to the completion of the railroad from Omaha, the origin of the Union Pacific, westward toward California were daunting. Dodge had to supply equipment, sustenance, and protection for approximately fifteen thousand men, including the surveyors, graders, scrapers, carpenters, and track layers, and hire foremen to supervise the construction.

Dodge immediately set up the workers, mostly veterans of the Civil War, for the railroad on a military structure. Because the Sioux and the Cheyenne, angered by the disruption of the

---

The obstacles to the completion of the railroad lines were daunting.

Great Plains buffalo herd and the encroachment upon their territories, repeatedly attacked and killed workers and raided their cattle and supplies, Dodge armed all workers and hired the Pawnees as armed scouts.

Dodge organized teams who laid an average of one to three miles of track per day and, at one stretch, more than eight miles in one day. The number of miles crossed is astonishing. In 1865, 40 miles of track had been laid; in 1866, after Dodge's influence, 260; and in 1867, 240, which included the ascent to the summit of the Rocky

Mountains, at an elevation of 8,235 feet. From 1868 until May 1869, 555 miles of track were laid, excluding almost 200 miles of temporary track.

All the supplies—locomotives, rails, spikes, ties, sledgehammers, shovels, rope, and rifles—were shipped from the East by steamboat, wagon, and eventually rail on tracks just laid. There were no bridges over the Missouri River, so transport across it depended upon the depth of the river.

Dodge scheduled work according to the weather, including the horrendous winter of 1866–67. In Nebraska, temperatures dropped to forty degrees below zero; the Missouri River stayed frozen until April. During February and March of 1867, construction halted completely. One man wrote, "We are out of luck in this country, wind blowing and snow drifting worse than ever, half the men either blind or frozen, looks bad." In April, Dodge pledged to complete "two miles a day for the first one hundred working days after the frost is out of the ground."

Except for the settlement at Salt Lake City, there were no towns or farms, and often no water sources or trees for wood, on the more than 1,087 miles where the line was built.

Grenville Mellen Dodge. Photograph provided by Union Pacific Historical Collection, Union Pacific Railroad Museum, Council Bluffs, Iowa.

NAME: Grenville Mellen Dodge

BORN: August 12, 1831, Danvers, Massachusetts

DIED: January 3, 1916

ACCOMPLISHMENTS: Chief Engineer for the building of the transcontinental railroad

QUOTATION: "I must push west."

In addition to organizing the men and these tasks, Dodge continued to lead the survey teams and select routes in advance of the construction—in 1867, covering more than 1400 miles in one two-month period. He also had to convince board members and politicians of the feasibility of his decisions.

From a dramatic rescue of a survey team who had been without water for more than a week on Wyoming's Red Desert to the establishment of law and order in the temporary towns that appeared along the railroad's bases, Dodge had responsibilities that were enormous.

"The great Pacific railway for California hail, bring on the locomotive, lay down the iron rail."
—Popular Song

General Sherman had predicted that building the railroad would be the "work of giants." Grenville Dodge maintained his integrity and repeatedly proved his reliability, his personal strength and courage, and his dedication to finishing the last major engineering project completed "by hand." He was truly a giant among powerful men.

When the engines of the Union Pacific and the Central Pacific met at Promontory Summit in 1869, Bret Harte wrote in a poem that the engines had "half a world behind each back." And Grenville Dodge, friend to generals and presidents, had led thousands of men to this day, uniting a country by uniting a continent.

Just for Two
Beverly McLoughland

Seesaw's thoughts
Are just for two—
Grass green
And sky blue,

Seesaw low
And seesaw high,
Bump the grass
And nudge the sky,

Trade each other
Green for blue—
Seesaw's thoughts
Are just for two.

Friendship
Carolyn Herrmann

Friendship is a treasure chest
Of golden memories,
Where two hearts share the riches
And understanding holds the keys.
And if each heart deposits
Lovely thoughts and actions here,
The treasure grows more valuable
With every passing year.

Hideaway
Mary Catherine Johnson

Peering through the swaying grace
Of green and amber willow lace
That curtains off our secret place,
	We survey the world with pride.

Our mothers search, but do not see
Our dancing eyes, nor hear our glee
Behind the fronds of willow tree,
	Where we most delight to hide.

My childhood friend of long ago,
If some wayward wind should blow
Us back to where those willows grow,
	Would you join me there inside?

*Roaring Brook flows past the brilliant autumn foliage in Baxter State Park,
Maine. Photograph by Mary Liz Austin/Donnelly Austin Photography.*

FOR THE CHILDREN

FRIENDS

Eileen Spinelli

I hear a car.
I hear a train.
I hear the splashing of the rain.
I hear my squeaky toy giraffe. . . .
I wish that I could hear you laugh.

I see the door.
I see the clock.
I see my little brother's sock.
I see a game we used to play. . . .
I don't see you—you moved away.

I touch my dog.
I touch the wall.
I touch the stone I found last fall.
I touch a shell still glistening sand. . . .
I wish that I could touch your hand.

You promised that
You'd phone me soon.
I sit and wait all afternoon.
When suddenly I hear a ring.
I hear my heart; it wants to sing.
I hear your voice, I hear you say:
"May I come visit Saturday?"

A loyal, furry friend attempts to console his young mistress in SYMPATHY, a painting by Briton Riviere (1840–1920). Image from Fine Art Photographic Library, Ltd., London.

Little Friend
Marty Hale

My dreams were crumbled, my house
Of cards came tumbling down,
And all my bright air-castles
Had fallen to the ground.
I swore there was no loyalty,
Friendship was a myth, and so
I'd never trust in them again;
My lovely dreams must go.

And then I heard the pat of paws,
The click of little toes,
And in my hand there snuggled close
A little cold, wet nose.

Laugh!
Nick Kenny

A laugh is a smile set to music,
So laugh and make life worth the while.
The philosophers say
That a chuckle a day
Has medicine beaten a mile.

Life's friendliest thing is a puppy;
He breaks down the coldest of hearts.
When he kisses your hand,
It means "I understand,"
And that's when the ice-breaking starts.

Just copy that four-legged rascal;
Treat life with a heart-warming grin.
Laugh at blizzard and squall,
For no reason at all,
And watch how the sunshine steals in.

To a Dog
Paul Leland McConomy

I had a friend with soft, brown eyes,
Staunch loyalty, and stately tread.
For when the sun had climbed the skies
And August's fitful breeze had fled,
We walked the silent, woodland aisles—
A realm of shadows, dark and cool.
And she would practice canine wiles
On sylvan scents and sounds. The pool,
The arching tree, and dragonfly
Were her delight, and she was part
Of that primordial ecstasy
And of the wildwood's beating heart.
Forgotten in that pleasant glen
Were all the human cant and lies,
The shattered loyalty of men.
I had a friend with soft, brown eyes.

Duty
Maxine Brown Phillips

The dog has cares:
He notes our doings with a close concern;
Monitors each going, each return;
Challenges all comers to the door
With balanced blend of wag and roar.
Post- and meter men are warned of doing wrong;
Squirrels are kept in trees where they belong.
Dogs not native to the block are put to rout;
And when, at night, the books are closed and laid aside,
Light switch snapped and good-night word exchanged,
Pillows flattened and covers all arranged,
He groans and stretches on his rug, close by,
Then heaves a long and deeply thankful sigh.

Two Brittany puppies await an invitation to play.
Photograph by Daniel Dempster.

Ravelry
Olive Breed

A little, ring-tailed, blue-eyed, golden ball
Of kitten bounds upon the easy chair
And, soft and fluffy, manages to fall
Into some prized, unfinished knitting there.

How charmed the bright, exploratory eyes!
How quickly velvet sheath reveals a claw
Quite sharp and curved enough and of a size
To pull out yarn and wind it round each paw.

If life could be unraveled with such ease
For my re-patterning, then I might know
Just half the joy my playful kitten sees
In tearing out my knitting, row by row.

A Cat Can Fit
Bonnie Highsmith Taylor

There's no box too small for a cat;
No matter how tiny, he'll fit.
There is no hole he can't slip through,
No shelf too narrow to sit.

There is no tree he cannot climb,
The taller, the higher he'll go.
There is no attic he can't explore,
No cellar, no matter how low.

There is no person a cat can't own,
No heart that a cat can't win—
No matter how hard, no matter how tight,
A cat will squeeze his way in.

A young girl holds her beloved friend close to her heart. Photograph by Alan Pitcairn/Grant Heilman Photography.

First Kitten

Elise Barese

We met one sunny August day;
Wide-eyed with wonder, you came to stay.
Fragile pixie, warm pocket sprite,
Dark tiger patches on snowy white,

Pink button-nose, moist like dew,
Eyes bright orbs of heavenly blue—
I lost my heart to your kitten face.
You've made our home a brighter place.

It is a very inconvenient habit of kittens (Alice had once made the remark) that, whatever you say to them, they always purr.
—LEWIS CARROLL

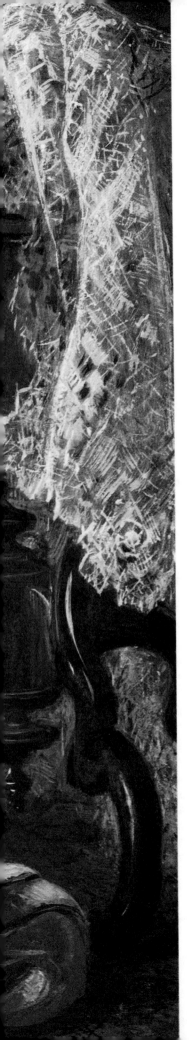

Song to a Siamese Cat

Joan C. Westcott

I have a little shadow
That follows wherever I go;
She's nothing but a wisp of fur
With great blue eyes aglow.
But she loves me with all her heart,
And I love her with mine,
And a closer friendship has not been seen
Since days of auld lang syne.

Loving hearts are not confined
To our floundering human race,
And here in a tiny kitten's eyes we see
A reflection of God's ever-shining grace.

Packages

Mary Wheeler Edgerton

They thank us in so many ways:
With paw or wagging tail,
With eyes that pledge devotion,
And love that will not fail.

How silent would the world have been
Without a cheery bark or purr,
Without God's gift of friendship
Wrapped in packages of fur.

Cuddles

Victoria H. B. Widry

A warm, soft
Ball of silky fur
Pleads to me with hazel eyes,
A message in her purr.

She watches every move I make,
Hoping I sit down.
It doesn't matter what I wear,
Old housedress or a gown.

On me, she curls into a muff
Then sighs and takes her nap,
But meows because, when I stand up,
I take away her lap.

*These precious kittens are making mischief in elegant surroundings,
despite their mother's watchful eye, in this painting, MISCHIEF
MAKERS, by Henriette Ronner Knip (1821–1909). Image from Fine
Art Photographic Library, Ltd., London/Private Collection.*

SLICE OF LIFE

Edna Jaques

AS TIME GOES ON

As time goes on, we gather up
    A hundred little odds and ends:
A pretty cup we like to use,
    A parting gift from old-time friends,
A scalloped plate with roses on,
    A handkerchief of snowy lawn.

As time goes on, we plant a tree
    Or tend a child with loving care,
Take part in something in the church,
    Win ribbons at a country fair,
Knit socks for someone overseas,
    Rub ointment on a small boy's knees.

As time goes on, we learn to think
    In ways that take in all mankind;
Hearts soften up and we take on
    A new serenity of mind.
We grow more tolerant, I guess,
    Think more, expect a little less.

As time goes on, if we be true,
    We lean on peace and kindness more;
Old truths take on a finer glow;
    We tend to set a higher store
On simpler things; pretense and pride,
    Like outworn styles, are set aside.

Thus in humility we move
Down ever-widening aisles of love.

Farewell to Summer

George Arnold

Summer is fading; the broad leaves that grew
So freshly green, when June was young, are falling;
And, all the whisper-haunted forest through,
The restless birds in saddened tones are calling,
From rustling hazel copse and tangled dell,
    "Farewell, sweet Summer,
    Fragrant, fruity Summer,
    Sweet, farewell!"

Upon the windy hills, in many a field,
The honeybees hum slow, above the clover,
Gleaning the latest sweets its blooms may yield,
And, knowing that their harvest time is over,
Sing, half a lullaby and half a knell,
    "Farewell, sweet Summer,
    Honey-laden Summer,
    Sweet, farewell!"

The little brook that babbles mid the ferns,
O'er twisted roots and sandy shallows playing,
Seems fain to linger in its eddied turns
And with a plaintive, purling voice is saying
(Sadder and sweeter than my song can tell),

    "Farewell, sweet Summer,
    Warm and dreamy Summer,
    Sweet, farewell!"

The fitful breeze down the winding lane
With gold and crimson leaves before it flying;
Its gusty laughter has no sound of pain,
But in the lulls it sinks to gentle sighing
And mourns the summer's early broken spell,
    "Farewell, sweet Summer,
    Rosy, blooming Summer,
    Sweet, farewell!"

So bird and bee and brook and breeze make moan,
With melancholy song their loss complaining.
I too must join them, as I walk alone
Among the sights and sounds of Summer's waning.
I too have loved the season passing well,
    So, farewell Summer,
    Fair but faded Summer,
    Sweet, farewell!

Two friends contemplate the ageless pastime of puddle-jumping in Riverway Park, Boston, Massachusetts. Photograph by Dianne Dietrich Leis/Dietrich Leis Stock Photography.

COUNTRY CHRONICLE

Lansing Christman

SEPTEMBER'S SLOW FAREWELL

September is the quiet friend that leads us toward the bounty of autumn. The harsh heat of August becomes a more comforting warmth under the glow of a golden sun. Never mind that the hours of sunlight are not as long as they were in June and that occasional evenings have that touch of coolness that requires a light sweater.

The plants of the earth take advantage of the diminishing daylight hours and seem to exhibit a preference for dressing up in their finest, most elaborate attire in preparation for the season's last party.

> *The pace of every living thing has increased slightly, as if, once a maple leaf becomes a jewel, the signal for a celebration has occurred.*

The frosts will come, and autumn's colors are already beginning to show up across the hills. There is the scarlet of the sumac leaves painting the thin slope of the pasture on the knoll above the barns. The red of the woodbine brightens old stone walls, and the orange berries of the bittersweet dance in reflected sunlight.

The busy sounds of preparation for fall are varied. The squirrels and chipmunks begin their harvest in the hickories and butternuts. The dropped husks crackle under my footsteps as I take my afternoon walk. Crickets are chirping, too, offering a rhythmic tremolo befitting the closing of summer and autumn's arrival. Birds are singing again—morning, noon, and afternoon. The indigo buntings have taken over the lunchtime chorus, and the flickers have begun to gather in groups, almost as if they understand "the more, the merrier."

The pace of every living thing has increased slightly, as if, once a maple leaf becomes a jewel, the signal for a celebration has occurred and all life joins in the fun.

The stars are more brilliant, and there is a mellowness in the moonlit evenings that seems to be reminding us in a quiet way that these times spent relaxing outdoors may soon be shortened. The signs of the elaborate autumn harvest are on every farm and in every market, but more will come.

September's visit seems to quickly end as the invitation to welcome the brilliant arrival of autumn comes; but she remains a gentle friend that reminds us of beauty in the process of slow changes.

The author of four books, Lansing Christman has contributed to IDEALS *for more than thirty years. Mr. Christman has also been published in several American, international, and braille anthologies. He lives in rural South Carolina.*

This tree-lined lane in New Harbor, Maine, displays the brilliant colors of autumn. Photograph by Dick Dietrich/Dietrich Leis Stock Photography.

Dear Old School Friends

Fairy Walker Lane

I love to go back down sweet memory lane
And enjoy friends from my childhood terrain.
As I march down the path of the past, long ago,
I think of each one that I used to know
And remember them all and love them all still,
Who laughed and played in the school on the hill.

We shared our joys and we shared our sorrows;
We talked and planned for the great tomorrows.
Now I enjoy anew our laughter and play
In the so-long-ago, on a September day.
What pleasure it is to travel at will
And visit once more the school on the hill.

School Bells

LaVerne P. Larson

The bells are ringing once again,
So important to our land;
They have a special meaning for
Those who carry books in hand.

School is now in session;
Time to learn anew,
As the minds and hearts of youth
Bid vacation time adieu.

Lasting friendships will be gained
And knowledge, like a treasure;
School bells are the voice of truth
And hope beyond all measure.

*Echoes remain of students who once piled into these
two-hundred-year-old desks in Eureka Schoolhouse,
the oldest schoolhouse in Vermont.
Photograph by William H. Johnson.*

Class Reunion

Isabelle Lane Partise

We pause a moment at the door
While eager hearts race on ahead.
We long to follow on swift feet,
But walk with dignity instead.

We meet again as old friends do,
At first constrained by passing years;
But classmates' faces soon take form,
And hand clasps hand amid brief tears.

The slim, young girls are matrons now;
The boys are men grown older, gray.
But each has lived a rich, full life
And gained in stature in his way.

Some paths have crossed to meet again;
Some stars have dimmed and burn no more.
On some, success has left its mark,
And some show sorrows that they bore.

A stealthy glance at printed name
Brings youthful image fresh to mind;
A metamorphosis takes place
That glows upon a face that's lined.

And suddenly the years recede;
The time between has ceased to be;
And we are classmates once again,
The carefree friends we used to be.

*A divided road in Potawatomi State Park,
Door County, Wisconsin, is surrounded by lovely
autumn foliage. Photograph by Darryl R. Beers.*

83

DEVOTIONS FROM THE HEART

Pamela Kennedy

My command is this: Love each other as I have loved you. Greater love has no one than this, that he lay down his life for his friends. You are my friends if you do what I command. —*John 15:12–14* (NIV)

BEING GOD'S FRIEND

I recently attended a highly publicized debate at a nearby state university. It was between two college professors, one an atheist and the other a believer. The subject for the evening was: "Does God Exist?" The auditorium was so packed that an overflow crowd of almost a hundred people had to listen from the outer courtyards.

Fortunately I arrived early and found a seat near the front of the room. From there I could not only hear the responses of each man but see his facial expressions as well. They took turns, under a very strictly organized format, as each presented a point-by-point defense of his position, making a reasoned argument complete with computerized slides and graphics. Then they exchanged challenges and responses with one another.

Some of their premises were easy to follow, but others were complicated trails of logic that left many of us in the audience with furrowed brows. Things heated up at times, and there were a few sarcastic remarks tossed back and forth as well. When the two experts finished, there was a question-and-answer time, and several in the audience lined up to have a crack at their favorite debater.

It was an interesting evening, and I have to say I came away thinking the believer won hands down, but I wondered as I drove home if God had been very impressed with the whole thing.

It seems to me that, while it may be an interesting intellectual exercise to debate the existence of God, when we are all finished it really does not matter very much what we decide. It is a

---

Dear Lord, I thank You that You have already offered to be my friend. Help me to respond to Your love by learning to imitate You in my attitudes, actions, and words. Amen.

---

bit like debating the existence of gravity. We can compose clever arguments against it, but, in the end, when we drop our neatly bound thesis, it is still going to end up on the floor!

I find it interesting that nowhere in the Bible does Jesus debate or argue for the existence of God. Instead, He continually explains, in clear and simple terms, the way we can come closer to Him. Why is it then that we spend so much time doing just the opposite? We humans love to find loopholes, to seek contradictions, and to tease out elegant arguments, but we wind up where we began, just as isolated and lonely as ever.

When Jesus talked with His disciples one day, He addressed this tendency of humans to try to exist apart from God. He talked about a vine and its branches and about our remaining close to Him. And then in three simple sentences, He gave His followers the clear and concise formula for ending loneliness: if we would love each other the way He loved us, we would be His friends. Imagine that! We have the opportunity to become God's friends. We don't have to live in isolation or intellectual confusion. We don't have to defend God or create complicated arguments to prove His existence. We just have to copy Him, and He promises us we will be His friends.

How do we do that? What does it look like to copy God? For starters we forgive others who have wronged us, giving up our right to seek revenge. We reach out to the poor and needy in practical ways, without any thought of repayment or recognition. We stop judging others just because they are different from us in appearance or customs or

Maple leaves and ivy decorate the forest floor at Cave Hill, Louisville, Kentucky. Photograph by Daniel Dempster.

dress. We seek peace instead of confrontation, swallow our pride instead of insisting upon our own way, and listen with our hearts, not just our ears. Then we will enjoy the privilege of being called God's friends. Then we will never need to be lonely again.

READERS' FORUM

Snapshots from our IDEALS readers

Right: "Buddy-Boy" is a friendly lapful for Becca Murray, granddaughter of Don and Margarita Messersmith of Silver Spring, Maryland.

Below: Verna Larson of Fairfield Bay, Arkansas, shares this photograph of her grandchildren, three-year-old Lauren and one-year-old Braden, having "fun in the bathtub."

Below left: Five-year-old Meghan Tindel likes to help her grandmother, Carolyn Kelley, of Tampa, Florida, with her garden when she is not out fishing with her "PaPa."

Below right: Jordan Nicholson adores her "three little fishes" outfit, according to her great-grandmother, Valeria Richard of Moss Point, Mississippi. Jordan's parents, who live in Mobile, Alabama, will soon be instructing her in the art of fishing, a family pastime.

Right: Three-year-old Kennedy Mae Hart is holding an armful of love named "Mitsy." Kennedy Mae is the daughter of Kenny and Carol Hart of Hickory, North Carolina. Her great-grandmother, Carolyn Craig, and her grandmother, Wanda Heffner, shared this photograph with *Ideals.*

Below left: Young Tristan Alexander Kohn is surrounded by cuddly, soft friends in his own basket. Tristan lives in Tulsa, Oklahoma, but visits his great-grandmother, Dorothy Todd, in St. Louis, Missouri, often.

Below right: Three-year-old Megan Bikel of Palm Beach Gardens, Florida, is playing with a very patient friend. She is the great-granddaughter of Ann McChesney, of Black Mountain, North Carolina.

Thank you for sharing your family photographs with IDEALS. *We hope to hear from other readers who would like to share snapshots with the* IDEALS *family. Please include a self-addressed, stamped envelope if you would like the photos returned. Keep your original photographs for safekeeping and send duplicate photos along with your name, address, and telephone number to:*

Readers' Forum
Ideals Publications
535 Metroplex Drive, Suite 250
Nashville, Tennessee 37211

Below left: Emma Tarkelson is a cheerful gardener at her home in Chugiak, Alaska. It is not too cold to have a garden there, her grandmother, Berneta Lehman, of Berne, Indiana, informs us.

Below right: An expert tree climber, Emily Grace Prichard, daughter of Jeff and Kathy Prichard of Oceana, West Virginia, practices when she visits her grandparents, Arnold and Phyllis Sizemore, in nearby Fairdale.

ideals

Publisher, Patricia A. Pingry
Editor, Marjorie L. Lloyd
Designer, Marisa Calvin
Copy Editor, Melinda Rathjen
Permissions Editor, Patsy Jay
Contributing Writers, Lansing Christman, Maud Dawson, Pamela Kennedy, Melissa Lester, D. Fran Morley, Jackie Paschall, and Lisa Ragan

ACKNOWLEDGMENTS

BACHER, JUNE MASTERS. "Great Art of Kindness" and "Old Friendships." Used by permission of George W. Bacher. EHRMAN, EVA N. "Sprinkling Cans." Used by permission of George R. Ehrman. JAQUES, EDNA. "As Time Goes On" from *The Golden Road*, published by Thomas Allen, Ltd, 1953. Used by permission of Louise Bonnell. JARRELL, MILDRED. "Granny's Quilts." Used by permission of Serena Naumann. LARSON, LAVERN P. "School Bells." Used by permission of Maureen E. Walsh. RUDBERG, GERTRUDE. "Enduring Friends." Used by permission of Marjorie Weinstein, Trustee. SATHOFF, CRAIG E. "For a Friend." Used by permission of Mary L. Sathoff. SELLERS, BETTIE M. "Star Light, Star Bright" from *Spring Onions and Cornbread.* Copyright ©1978. Used by permission of Pelican Publishing Company, Inc. SCHLOMANN, LYNDA. "Summer Symphony." Used by permission of Julie Schlomann. Our sincere thanks to the heirs, whom we were unable to locate, of: Sylvia Trent Auxier for "Rendezvous" from *Love-Vine*, 1932, The Story Book Press; and Louise Driscoll for "Mid-August" from *Garden Grace,* 1924, MacMillan Co. We thank those authors, or their heirs, some of whom we were unable to locate, who submitted poems or articles to *Ideals* for publication. Every possible effort has been made to acknowledge ownership of material used.

The origins, traditions and customs of our holidays...
AMERICA CELEBRATES

Americans love a parade, with trumpets and trombones blaring, the color guard striding straight and tall, and the flag passing by in review. This could be in your town, or any town, on Independence Day, on Memorial Day, or even on Labor Day.

But there are other kinds of celebrations throughout our vast country as well: some filled with fun and gaiety, some with only family gathered round, others full of ancient tradition. *America Celebrates* is an invitation to experience, through tender poetry and touching articles, the customs, the memories, and the traditions of each of our most beloved holidays.

In addition to magnificent, full-color photographs, there are memory-evoking, vintage photographs that will remind you of some of your own snapshots from the years past and may even bring a tear to your eye.

You'll read about the origins of Father's Day, Mother's Day, and Thanksgiving Day, as well as the American customs added to the Old-World celebrations of Easter and Christmas.

Complete the Free Examination Certificate and mail today for your 21-Day Preview. You will receive a FREE *Moments to Celebrate* booklet just for ordering.

No need to send money now!

GOD is waiting to hear your . . .
praise, concerns, requests, dreams, worries & more!

Make Your Prayer Life the Best It's Ever Been With this Amazing New Book.

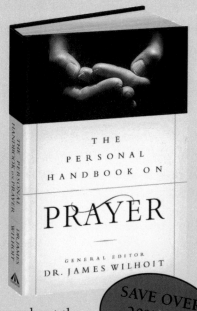

The Personal Handbook on Prayer has been designed to help you easily and joyfully explore the mystery and power of prayer, and shows you how you can enhance your prayer life every day. You'll take a closer look at the loving God to Whom we pray, the power of prayer, and the process of prayer.

The Personal Handbook on Prayer contains dozens of prayers from the Bible that have timeless power and relevance.

The Personal Handbook on Prayer offers dozens of "Prayer Starters" — you'll have everything you need to verbalize your needs, praise, and thanksgiving in prayer.

SAVE OVER 20% OFF Retail Price!

Throughout the book, you'll find an inspiring and delightful collection of quotes and tidbits that will amplify the text and lead you to greater joy in a life of prayer.

TRY THIS BOOK RISK-FREE FOR 30 DAYS!

- 6 ⅜" x 9 ¼" hardcover book with 320 pages of inspiring and practical articles, and exploration of every aspect of prayer.

- 100 fascinating articles on prayer written by some of today's best known Christian leaders.

- 50 major prayers of the Bible

- 130 "Prayer Starters."

- Complete with Topical, Scripture and Resource Indexes.

Only $18.96
payable in 2 installments of $9.48 each, plus shipping and processing.

❧ FREE EXAMINATION CERTIFICATE ❧

YES! I'd like to examine *The Personal Handbook on Prayer*, at no risk or obligation. If I decide to keep the book, I will be billed later at the low Guideposts price of only $18.96, payable in 2 installments of $9.48 each, plus shipping and processing. If not completely satisfied, I may return the book within 30 days and owe nothing. The FREE Prayer Reflection Cards are mine to keep no matter what I decide.

Total copies ordered: _____

Please print your name and address:

_____

NAME

_____

ADDRESS   APT#

_____

CITY   STATE   ZIP

Allow 4 weeks for delivery. Orders subject to credit approval.
Send no money now. We will bill you later.
www.guidepostsbooks.com

Printed in USA
11/202219503

YOUR FREE GIFT!
12 ENCOURAGING PRAYER REFLECTIONS CARDS
(2 OF EACH CARD)
No need to send money now!